Meditations for the Dead and Dying

By Perry Gasteiger

abuddhapress@yahoo.com

Acknowledgements

First and foremost, thank you to my wickedly talented and disgustingly brilliant editor — and sister — Maglyn Gasteiger. I wouldn't be anywhere without you.

Thank you to Red and Alien Buddha Press for taking a chance on my work. You have been nothing short of wonderful to worth with.

Thank you Ryan for having the utmost faith in my abilities and never letting me give up on myself.

And thank you mom, for everything.

ISBN: 9798471454620

Growing Pains

—after *I Sing the Body Electric; Especially When My Power Is Out*

Like a snake, I shed the skin
you so graciously shoved me into:
molting this visage
gifted to me in your benevolence,
my body grows too bold
for the mold in which you encase me.
Angry fissures spider-web
over my body in fractured magnificence,
hatching from my porcelain prison
I rise through the wreckage,
jagged edges catching fresh pink skin,
raking flaming valleys filled with shadows
into broken arms, rippling muscles
bulging under tattered limbs
aching to taste freedom from their cells.
My spine stands sharp,
ripping the seams sewn too tight to breathe,
ribs creaking and cracking
as you take me in a few more inches,
thin skin stretched tight across shoulders
painted red with thrown away words:
(mea culpa, mea culpa)

your tongue strikes deep,
but my blood runs deeper,
bursting through lacerations,
pouring forth from my pores;
it drips from my mouth as I scream in release,
waves of pain crashing against delicate flesh
as cruel ecstasy throbs in every nerve:
it hurts to become.

Corpus Corallium

I drag her coral skeleton through the sand,
laying out the pieces phalanx by phalanx,
tibia to femur, vertebrae stacked,
topped with a pockmarked skull;

I pull strands of seaweed from silt beds,
weaving them into her crown,
singing as I place each lock,
braiding seashells and fish bones into her hair;

I reach into the mouth of a great white shark,
rip out its beating heart and watch his brothers
descend upon his bloodied body,
wade back through the waves to place it
lovingly between her ribs,
affix delicate jellyfish tendril veins
watching as life begins to pulse through her;

I watch her rise, dripping in
ocean tears and blood,
reach to her to embrace
that which I had brought to be,
fall to my knees and weep,
sinking into soft sand
as she crawls toward the sea
from which I stole her.

Apricots

She sinks her teeth into
a tender apricot, sticky-sweet
juice drips down her chin
like rushing waterfalls pouring
into the crevices of her skin,
gathering in lakes and rivers,
sugared and thick with syrupy kisses
and honey soaked bodies.

She tears at bruised flesh
watching bit by bit devoured
by glistening lips longing for more,
to rip from the pit that supple thing
which finds its bed in the suffering
of tender fruit sucked dry,
left husked and spent
in the palms of indulgent hands.

She carefully places the stone
in my open mouth,
seals it with a kiss and watches
roots grow from my toes,
branches crack my ribs,
a canopy burst from my crown
in beautiful becoming,
blooming with tender violence.

She sits beneath the shade of my leaves,
my boughs heavy with unclaimed fruits
waiting for her starving mouth.
She cannot resist
the smell of fresh nectar —
licking her lips as she
reaches up and plucks
another tender apricot.

A Snack in the Sunshine

You lay there asleep under the willow tree,
I hear the carrion birds calling
hungry songs into the dawn,
wretched screeches as they beat their wings
and descend upon your body.
I hear flesh tear from bone like
sweet babes from mothers' wombs —
my stomach rumbles at your carcass
stripped down to ivory nakedness,
baring itself to the rising sun
the bits not worth scavenging rot
under the hot glare of the day.
I crack a bone and suck the marrow,
the smell of putrid matter fills my nostrils
and I breathe deep, licking my fingers
sitting in the shade of the willow tree —
a child screams and I fall asleep
thinking of you in the fragrant heat.

A Modest Feast

Perverse conductors
of power and gain
gorge themselves on our bodies,
licking bloodied chops
as they stare down at our skeletons
dancing on gilt strings,
jeweled chains hanging loosely
from chipped ankles
as we lurch and clatter
into piles of spent ivory.

Our minds were stained
by the machination of our lives,
and it is our time to feast;
to sate starving stomachs,
cut our teeth on gold-plated bones
as we tear at soft flesh,
chewing fat until it sticks
to our tongues,
coating our palettes
thick with rebellious words.

We burned their factories,
danced in the flames, and at bloody dawn
they stuck their heads in piles of ashes
as hungry armies of the not-quite-dead
spilled over the horizon:
they never saw us coming.

Blood and Body
--after *Howl*

We walked all night
with shoes full of blood,
and at dawn cast them off
to dance barefoot over rocks
with iron-stained faces
bearing our naked soles
and uncalloused toes.

Arches fall, tendons collapsing
under the weight of standing reverent,
bones grind to dust
inside the folds of our skin
and we crawl on knees rubbed raw,
gouge palms on jagged stone
as prostrations shatter
what's left of tattered limbs.

Mangled trunks inch forward like worms
writhing on warm pavement,
rolling onto sun-blistered backs,
praying to an empty sky until
we bite off our tongues,
leaving us choking in fountains
of our own transubstantiation.

Elegy on a Highway

Stumbling down the road barefoot
with battered daisies clenched
in my fists, tears on my tongue
and dirt packed into open wounds --
I'm thinking about walking down
main street with him.
You know, I used to be so pretty,
dripped from the inside
with sunshine and honey
blowing kisses across the sidewalk.

Running down the road bloody
my abdomen throbbing,
stomach heaving with
the effort of not spilling
right out onto the black tar --
I'm thinking about sunshine,
how it burns if you keep it caged,
that honey sticks to pieces that sting,
and how quickly a kiss turns into a scream.

Racing down the road ragged
with rocks in my teeth, gravel in my cheek
and blood running down my thigh
staining the hem of my dress --
I'm thinking about flowers wilting
on the kitchen table, my eyes
empty, staring at the wall
and how the world caves in
when no one is looking.

Collapsing on the road, taken and spent,
my body doubling on itself with remembrance
gasping for air, listening to the blissful ignorance
of the cicadas --
I'm thinking about white sheets
on a bed that's mine, and an alarm clock
ringing in the rest of my life,
about sunshine and honey
and the hollow left behind.

Ode to Re-Becoming

She wanders through a wasted land,
callous beams throwing fists of needles
into the backs of her retinas,
sunburned dunes scorching her toes.

Her nose slides down her face,
the tang of iron painting her lips
as bloody cartilage explodes
into sprawling mountains at her feet.

Soft blue veins split open
like velvet tearing at the seams,
spilling oceans into the sand,
pooling in the tracks behind her.

Swollen eyes burst in their sockets,
viscous humor streaking her cheeks,
dripping from her chin in jelly droplets,
gouging valleys in the ground before her.

Teeth rot from the roots,
falling from her gaping mouth,
seeding the earth in her wake,
growing great trunks from their cavities.

Skin peels away in chunks
carpeting the ground,
muscles melt off the bone
molding new life in the cradle of dead flesh.

And she is left stripped,
naked:
a skeleton rattling
in her luscious creation.

Lochia

We are borne from the marrow
of the skeleton of the universe:
she taps a femur and lets it crack,
dripping sweetness onto earth --
thick droplets, sticky and potent,
crash to the ground.
She takes us tenderly,
unmolded
between her fingertips,
pressing us into bodies
we never asked to know.

Stars fall from the sky like tears
shattering into a thousand radiant fragments
at our newfound feet,
slicing our soles as we dance
breathlessly before our mother.
She sings to us in tongues
infinite vibrations rattling our bones,
shaking loose our teeth and kneecaps,
disjointed:
tendons snap and cartilage pops
and bodies rupture at resonant frequency.

She reclaims the life she bled into us
and we rest, once again nestled into her hollows.

New Leaves

I love new leaves

& the smell of blood as life tumbles forward
tearing into the world from heaving wombs
umbilical cords wrapped around slender necks
as young lungs struggle to take their first breath

& cherry blossoms opening in fragrant spring
impatient heads crowning through fragile buds
bursting forth in brutal inception,
thin seals wrenched open with ignorant disregard

& red stains upon pink skin, tender and screaming
as fresh air rakes its nails along naked nerves,
the remnants of a torn vessel cling to raw flesh
glistening in the carnage left in the wake of creation

& sweet sap bleeding through cracked bark
flowing free through valleys gouged into faces
of unwavering trunks, splitting as new growth
forces its way into the world, green and sticky

& the violence and beauty of becoming,
witnessing the sight of a child
ripped from the stomach of its mother
leaving her stretched and hollow and bloody

there really is nothing more stunning than new leaves.

Perry Gasteiger is a queer, non-binary poet and writer from Ontario, Canada. Their current work embraces a Post-Modern Gothic sensibility, taking a keen interest in playing with a reader's discomfort to bring about an empathetic understanding of different aspects of the world. Perry enjoys exploring the banal darkness of our everyday world using juxtaposition between the real and the abstract, the beautiful and the deformed, the congruent and the disordered. With a distinct love for local art, and the impact it can have on its community, Perry has been working on their project "The Blank Page Initiative" to bring together local creators in fun and accessible ways in Southwestern Ontario. Perry is also an Editor at the Red Lemon Review, an online literary magazine that uplifts the mundane through unique perspectives. You can find their work in places such as Anti-Heroin Chic Magazine, Spellbinder Magazine, Fevers of the Mind, Not Deer Magazine, Outcast Press, Warning Lines Magazine, and Melbourne Culture Corner Magazine.

Connect with Perry at www.perrygasteiger.ca

or on Twitter at @sunshineloft

The Following Poems Were Previously Published:

A Snack in the Sunshine - Not Deer Magazine (August 2021)

Blood and Body - Not Deer Magazine (August 2021)

Ode to Re-Becoming - Not Deer Magazine (August 2021)

New Leaves - Outcast Press Poetry Vol 2 (August 2021)

Made in the USA
Middletown, DE
24 November 2021

53320225R00018